SPOOKY SITES

ST. AUGUSTINE LIGHTHOUSE

THOMAS KINGSLEY TROUPE

A Shark Book
SEAHORSE PUBLISHING

Teaching Tips for Caregivers:

You can help your child learn by encouraging them to read widely, both as a leisure activity and as a way of satisfying their curiosity about the world. Reading helps build a strong foundation in language and literacy skills that will help your child succeed in school. This high-interest book will appeal to all readers in intermediate and middle school grades.

Use the following suggestions to help your child grow as a reader.

- Encourage them to read independently at home.
- Encourage them to practice reading aloud.
- Encourage activities that require reading.
- Establish a regular reading time.
- Have your child ask and answer questions about what they read.

Teaching Tips for Teachers:

Engage students throughout the reading process by asking questions like these.

Before Reading

- Ask, "What do you already know about this topic?"
- Ask, "What do you want to learn about this topic?"

During Reading

- Ask, "What is the author trying to teach you?"
- Ask, "How is this like something you have read or seen before?"
- Ask, "How do the text features (headings, index, etc.) help you understand the topic?"

After Reading

- Ask, "What interesting or fun fact did you learn?"
- Ask, "What questions do you still have about the topic? How could you find the answers?"

TABLE OF CONTENTS

Bright Light, Dark Night 4
The History of St. Augustine Lighthouse 6
Paranormal Playground? 10
Not Just Ghostly Girls 14
Real or Hoax? 17
Paranormal Proof? 18
Be a Paranormal Investigator! 20
Glossary 22
Index 23
After Reading Questions 23
About the Author 24

Bright Light, Dark Night

It's dark and quiet inside the historic **lighthouse**. You're all alone. You want to reach the top, so you take the first step of the spiral staircase. Only 218 more steps to go. Your hand grips the railing. It's cold to the touch. Too cold. You find that strange since it's the middle of summer.

As you carefully ascend the steps, you hear something up above you. It sounds like a child laughing. That can't be. You're the only one here! With a shaky thumb, you click on your flashlight and move the beam up the winding stairs. A dark, faceless **apparition** looks down at you. You're not alone after all!

The History of St. Augustine Lighthouse

The St. Augustine Lighthouse is a beautiful old structure in St. Augustine, Florida. It sits on Anastasia Island and stands 165 feet (50 meters) above sea level. The lighthouse overlooks Matanzas Bay and the Atlantic Ocean.

Construction of the lighthouse began in 1871. It was built to replace an old Spanish **watchtower** that once stood there. A man named Hezekiah Pittee was chosen to oversee the construction. He moved onto the site along with his wife Mary and his children Mary, Eliza, Edward, and Carrie.

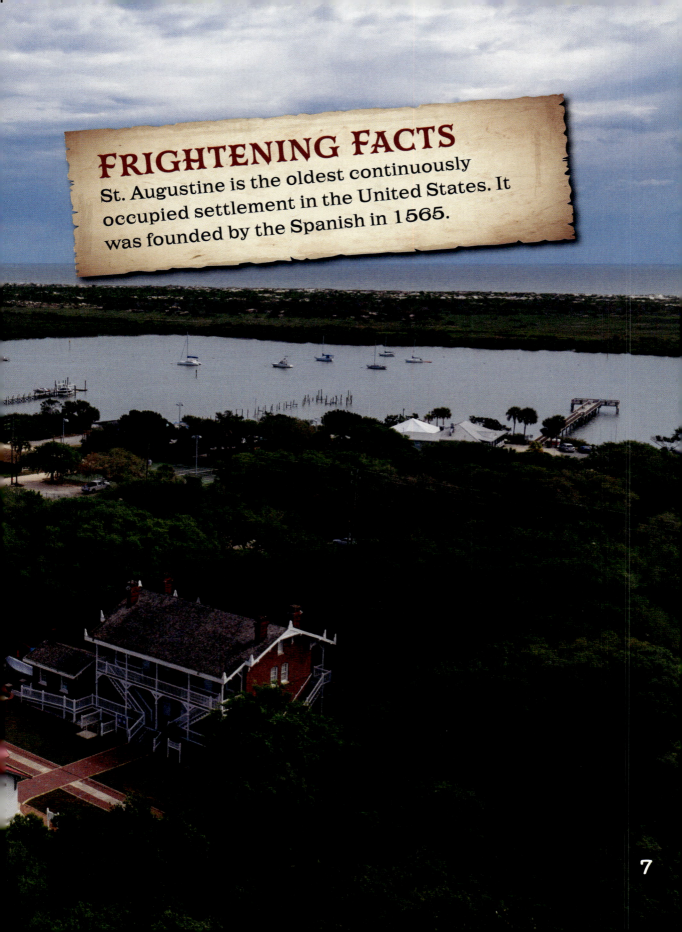

FRIGHTENING FACTS
St. Augustine is the oldest continuously occupied settlement in the United States. It was founded by the Spanish in 1565.

By 1873, only the **foundation** and 42 feet (13 meters) of the lighthouse's walls were complete. A railway was built to move materials from supply ships to the construction site. When work wasn't being done, the Pittee children liked to ride the rail cart down a hill. It was like an old-fashioned rollercoaster.

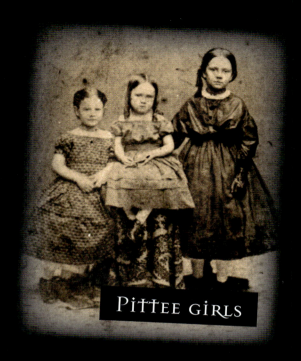

PITTEE GIRLS

A board at the end of the tracks was supposed to keep the cart from going into the water. But on July 10, 1873, the three Pittee girls, along with an unnamed friend, rode the cart to the end of the rails. The safety board was not in place. The cart flipped into the water, trapping the girls beneath it. A construction worker named Dan Sessions dove in to try and save the girls. Only the youngest, Carrie, survived.

Paranormal Playground?

The Pittees took the bodies of their girls back to their home state of Maine to be buried. Even so, some believe the girls' spirits never left the lighthouse. Visitors and tour guides report hearing ghostly giggling in the dark. When they search for the source of the noises, no one is there. Are the Pittee girls playing games...even in the **afterlife**?

A large brick building known as the keeper's house stands near the lighthouse. After construction on the lighthouse was completed in 1874, the workers who ran the lighthouse lived there.

Legend has it that a man who was sleeping in the keeper's house woke up in the middle of the night. He saw a small girl standing near his bed. When he blinked his eyes, she disappeared. Was this just one of many **paranormal** encounters that have happened at the site?

KEEPER'S HOUSE

In the woods near the St. Augustine Lighthouse, there are trails to explore. They give visitors a good look at the area's natural beauty...and maybe something unexpected!

One visitor to the trails claims to have seen a girl in **Victorian** dress sitting on a bench, reading a book. The hiker was about to talk to the girl when a tour group came by and distracted her. When she looked back to the bench again, the girl had completely vanished.

FRIGHTENING FACTS

The St. Augustine Lighthouse is still in operation today. Workers claim to find dirty, child-sized footprints on the floors. Are the Pittee girls still playing there?

Not Just Ghostly Girls

Just before Christmas in 1859, lighthouse keeper Joseph Andreu was painting the exterior of the building. Tragically, he fell from a great height and died. Afterward, his wife Maria is said to have climbed to the top of the lighthouse. She cried out, "What shall I do?" It's rumored that she heard the voice of her lost husband whispering through the wind to give her an answer: "Tend to the light."

Maria became the first Hispanic-American female lighthouse keeper in Florida. Though she didn't die at the lighthouse, many believe her ghost is there. People have seen Maria's image looking over the **catwalk**, down to where her husband Joseph fell.

FRIGHTENING FACTS

Lighthouse visitors sometimes smell cherry tobacco. It was a favorite of lighthouse keeper Peter Rasmussen, who watched the site for 23 years in the early 1900s. There's no smoking at the lighthouse today!

Maria Andreu

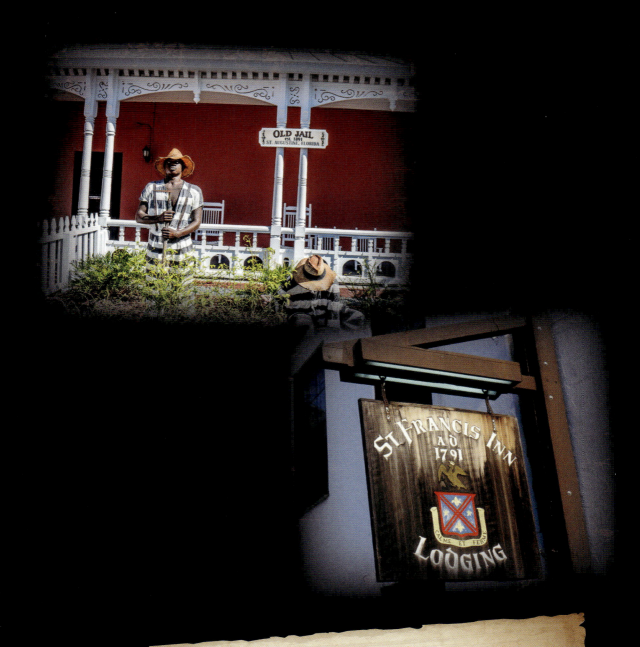

FRIGHTENING FACTS

The city of St. Augustine, Florida, is said to be one of the most haunted places in the country. Besides the lighthouse, other spooky sites include the Old Jail Museum, St. Francis Inn, and Casa de Suenos, a bed-and-breakfast that used to be a funeral home.

Real or Hoax?

Places that are rumored to be haunted draw many adventurous and curious people. Some of them get tired while climbing the long staircase up to the top of the St. Augustine Lighthouse. A few claim they have felt a hand on their back, urging them to keep going. When they turn to see who is helping them, there's no one there. It could be the help of a friendly spirit!

Is the lighthouse really haunted? Many believe it's possible. They argue that because so many tragic deaths have happened there, paranormal activity is likely. But there are also many **skeptics** who say it's all a **hoax**.

Paranormal Proof?

Paranormal investigators claim that the St. Augustine Lighthouse is a hotbed of haunted activity. Grant Wilson and Jason Hawes from TV's *Ghost Hunters* called the lighthouse "the Mona Lisa of paranormal sites."

Like other investigators, Wilson and Hawes use digital recorders to capture EVP (electronic voice phenomena). EVPs are audio recordings that are believed to be the words of the dead. Investigators also set up cameras to try and capture evidence of any **abnormal** shadow figures that appear at the site.

FRIGHTENING FACTS

Photos that seem to show a ghost peeking over the lighthouse stairs have been taken by visitors and investigators. Could it be one of the Pittee girls? Or a former lighthouse keeper?

Be a Paranormal Investigator!

Whether it's really haunted or not, the St. Augustine Lighthouse is still a creepy place to explore. It is open for tours. You can even take a night tour to see if something spooky happens during your visit!

Are the lost souls of the Pittee girls still playing games here? Do the old lighthouse keepers still watch over the waters? No one knows for sure.

Do you want to be a paranormal investigator? You can! All you really need is a flashlight, an audio recorder, and some bravery. Go to a dark, creepy place. Look around and ask questions. Record the whole EVP session. When you play the recording back, you might hear strange things. Is it something paranormal trying to talk to you? It could be!

Glossary

abnormal (ab-NOR-muhl): not normal; unusual

afterlife (AF-tur-life): an existence after the death of a person's physical body

apparition (ap-puh-RI-shuhn): a supernatural appearance of a person or thing; a ghost or specter

catwalk (KAT-wawk): a narrow, elevated walkway or platform

foundation (foun-DAY-shuhn): a solid structure on which a building is constructed

hoax (hohks): a trick that makes people believe something that is not true

lighthouse (LITE-hous): a tower in or near the sea with a flashing light at the top that helps ships avoid danger

paranormal (pair-uh-NOR-muhl): something that cannot be explained by science

skeptics (SKEP-tiks): people who have doubts or questions about whether something is true

Victorian (vik-TOR-ee-uhn): related to the rule of Queen Victoria in England in the mid- to late-1800s; a time when people wore corsets, bonnets, top hats, bustles, and petticoats

watchtower (WAHCH-tou-ur): a high tower that serves as a lookout

Index

Andreu, Joseph 14

Andreu, Maria 14, 15

evidence 18

EVP(s) 18, 21

ghost 14, 19

haunted 16–18, 20

Hawes, Jason 18

investigator(s) 18, 19, 21

Pittee girls 9, 10, 13, 19, 20

Pittee, Hezekiah 6

Rasmussen, Peter 15

Wilson, Grant 18

After Reading Questions

1. What happened to Joseph Andreu?

2. Why do you think the ghosts of the Pittee girls might want to stay at the lighthouse?

3. What are EVPs? What EVPs have been captured at the lighthouse?

4. What qualities of an old lighthouse make it a likely setting for ghost stories?

About the Author

Thomas Kingsley Troupe is the author of over 200 books for young readers. When he's not writing, he enjoys reading, playing video games, and investigating haunted places with the Twin Cities Paranormal Society. Otherwise, he's probably taking a nap or something. Thomas lives in Woodbury, Minnesota, with his two sons.

Written by: Thomas Kingsley Troupe
Design by: Under the Oaks Media
Editor: Kim Thompson

Photo credits: Carmen K. Sisson/Cloudybright / Alamy Stock Photo: P. 12; All other images from Shutterstock or in the public domain.

Library of Congress PCN Data
St. Augustine Lighthouse / Thomas Kingsley Troupe
Spooky Sites
ISBN 979-8-8904-2688-8 (hard cover)
ISBN 979-8-8904-2716-8 (paperback)
ISBN 979-8-8904-2744-1 (EPUB)
ISBN 979-8-8904-2772-4 (eBook)
Library of Congress Control Number: 2023923681

Printed in the United States of America.

Seahorse Publishing Company
seahorsepub.com

Copyright © 2025 **SEAHORSE PUBLISHING COMPANY**

All rights reserved. No part of this publication may be reproduced, stored in a retrieval system or be transmitted in any form or by any means, electronic, mechanical, photocopying, recording, or otherwise, without the prior written permission of Seahorse Publishing Company.

Published in the United States
Seahorse Publishing
PO Box 771325
Coral Springs, FL 33077